About the Author

Megan Costa is a passionate poetess and advocate whose debut poetry book *Life After* highlights the journey to healing after surviving sexual abuse. With a deep commitment to shedding light on the often-taboo subject of trauma, she uses her writing to explore the complexities of recovery, resilience and refinement. Through her work, Megan aims to promote healing in a world that desperately needs compassion. When she's not at work, she enjoys long walks with her best friend and curling up with her two dogs, a book and a blanket.

Life After

To Aimee (Shrek)

love Meg (shitface)
x

Megan Costa

Life After

Olympia Publishers
London

www.olympiapublishers.com
OLYMPIA PAPERBACK EDITION

Copyright © Megan Costa 2025

The right of Megan Costa to be identified as author of
this work has been asserted in accordance with sections 77 and 78 of
the Copyright, Designs and Patents Act 1988.

All Rights Reserved

No reproduction, copy or transmission of this publication
may be made without written permission.
No paragraph of this publication may be reproduced,
copied or transmitted save with the written permission of the publisher,
or in accordance with the provisions
of the Copyright Act 1956 (as amended).

Any person who commits any unauthorised act in relation to
this publication may be liable to criminal
prosecution and civil claims for damage.

A CIP catalogue record for this title is
available from the British Library.

ISBN: 978-1-83543-697-4

First Published in 2025

Olympia Publishers
Tallis House
2 Tallis Street
London
EC4Y 0AB

Printed in Great Britain

Dedication

To all those who had their choices taken away. I am proud of you for choosing to stay. May you continue to find your voice and reclaim your power, knowing that you are not alone in this journey.

Acknowledgements

I would like to extend my heartfelt gratitude to my incredible mum, whose unwavering support and love have been my foundation throughout this journey. Your strength and determination inspire me every day, and I am so grateful for the countless sacrifices you've made to help me pursue my dreams. To my sister, thank you for being my confidante and for always believing in me, even when I struggled to believe in myself. Your laughter has inspired me when things get tough, and your encouragement has pushed me to keep going when I felt like giving up. A special thank you to my therapist, Emily, whose guidance and compassion have helped me navigate the complexities of my emotions. Your insights and support have been instrumental in my healing process, and I truly appreciate your dedication to helping me find my voice and the confidence to turn my writing into a book. To Alex, thank you for being my rock. Your love and support have given me the strength to face challenges head-on. I am so grateful for all the evenings you have let me read my work out to you, never commenting with anything but praise and constructive criticisms. To my friends – your motivation and understanding have been invaluable. Each of you has played a unique role in my life, offering support, positivity and a listening ear. You have stood beside me through the darkest moments and celebrated the light, reminding me of the beauty that can emerge from pain. The best cheerleaders I could ask for.

This book is not just a reflection of the journey I am on but also a testament to the love and strength that surrounds me. I am forever grateful to each of you, and I hope this collection resonates with you as much as your support has resonated with me. Thank you, for never doubting me. Lastly, thank you to all at Olympia, who have allowed me to make this dream a reality. For believing the writing I have worked so hard on has the potential to help others and granted me the opportunity to extend my support to those who may need it.

Disclaimer

This book contains poetry that addresses themes of sexual abuse and trauma. This content may be triggering for some readers. I do not claim to represent the experiences of all survivors. If you or someone you know is struggling, please seek support from a qualified professional. Reader discretion is advised.

I am sorry to the girl who didn't believe she was enough. (29.01.22)

I do not recognise the person I have become, full of loathing and hostility. When did I learn to hate so easily in the world I grew up in?
(05.02.22)

I can feel the venom in my words before I aim them at you, and I am sorry, for they burn on my tongue and I just want them out.
(14.02.22)

I saw my future in you and all you saw was a reason to leave. When you had the audacity to break my heart in a way I hadn't known possible, did you hear the pieces ricochet from the ground?
Silly me, I fell hopelessly in love with you. You watched me fall, and you walked away.
(26.02.22)

I lie awake wondering if you knew how much of me you destroyed.
Every time I feel that I am on top of the world, you push me right back down to where I don't want to be.
How do you still manage to hurt me, breaking parts of me long after I thought I had nothing left to break?
(01.03.22)

Do you remember how light your heart felt before the weight of the world rested on your shoulders?
The darkness is taking over.
You will let it engulf you, until you are nothing more than a faded star – gone long before anybody has realised.
(08.03.22)

You dream of forever.
Sweetie, look at your past and those who have left you, whether they wanted to or not. You do not have forever painted into your future.
(10.03.22)

It almost swallows you up, like when you're falling asleep.
Surrounded by dark thoughts and lonely nights.
Only, I don't want to wake up from this slumber.
(21.03.22)

Everywhere hurts.
I used to revel in being alone, but now it hurts so badly I can't breathe. When did I get so dependent?
(29.03.22)

I am terrified of how my life will change when the ghosts of my past emerge.
(01.04.22)

How can I survive these waves of emotions all hitting me at once?
I feel like I'm drowning and I am too afraid to grab onto a life jacket.
I feel like I am watching myself struggle through this outside of my body – too far away to call out for help.
(07.04.22)

I have lived a lie, and now I must deal with the consequences. (07.04.22)

I have shattered the lives of the people closest to me, with the simplest of sentences that carry so much weight.
And now that it's out, you do not have the power to hurt me any more.
(13.04.22)

I do not expect people to understand the feelings that I felt; they were real in my heart.
I cannot explain how I thought I had lost an angel, when I was freed of something far worse.
(13.04.22)

Despite my silence taunting me that I was weak;
I knew that I had a strength inside of me that scared you.
The secret you made me keep felt like black tape. Stuck tightly across my mouth, suffocating me.
Now it's out, I can finally breathe, for the first time in years.
(15.09.22)

I am scared that this is the end, and there is nothing I can do to prevent it.
(15.10.22)

Do not forget the friends that stand beside you. Without any doubt in their minds that you are the one they want to support. Cherish them, they are few and far between.
(03.11.22)

I was at a point where I thought that telling people could only make the pain worse and, for the first few weeks, I was right. I was terrified that this was it, 'the relief' – the calm after the storm of telling everyone. But it wasn't.
The anxiety subsided, and I am supported by everyone who knows and loves me. The sky is peaceful after all.
(15.12.22)

I don't think that I can call you it any more.
I don't think it is right that I use such a term of endearment after what you became.
I am working at calling you by your name and not the title you have ruined.
(25.03.23)

I used to ask Mum for money to go shopping with my friends. My heart would drop when she said to ask you. I knew what that would entail; I knew you would pull me into a corner, a bathroom, a loft.
You'd tell me to 'sort you out', so you could 'repay' me.
A ten-pound note was all I was worth to you. Nothing more than a cheap thrill.
The irony is, after I made sure I was never alone with you again and you began to despise me, the words you enjoyed throwing around most were 'Slag, Slut, Whore'.
I wonder where I learnt those characteristics, *Dad*.
Sexual favours just so I could have a happy meal with my friends.
(28.03.2023)

Life is a weird concept.
You work so hard to get to a place called Society,
Then you have to continue working harder and harder each day to live in a house called acceptance.
After you've reached this place, you have to keep going, keep working and keep changing to keep up with the absurdity of society.
Strange, this thing called life, but we're all here; we're are all on that journey, scrambling our way to the house called acceptance in the gated community called society.
Although, sometimes, those gates just won't open, and if they don't?
Build a castle right outside the entrance, big enough for the whole of society to see. Grand enough to make them turn green with envy.
And secure enough to make you feel safe, even on your worst days, without having to ask for help.
On those days, when you feel that the journey to acceptance is just too far to travel on your own, too frightening to endure and far more hassle than it is worth, try to remember that you are not alone.
(02.04.2023)

Finally, I can see the lightness in your heart, as you do the things you have only dreamt of doing. You are happy.
(24.05.23)

Where have you been hiding?
Why have you waited so long to come out from the shadows?
Show me your beauty, little one, for it is gleaming,
And we could all use a little light.
(02.06.23)

My head and my heart are arguing – who is right? And who will win?
(21.06.23)

I am fed up of not liking who I am.
So I've been thinking that if someone can *think* they love me as I am, then I can't be that bad.
But I do not like myself.
Losing you has made me realise that I want to be better, for myself and for the person who is eventually willing to stay.
(10.07.2023)

This is right.
We both knew it.
It just hurts after all the time we spent fighting, just to realise we were fighting for ourselves and not for each other.
(13.07.2023)

You are *stronger* than the crippling anxiety you feel.
You just need to realise that you have the ability to overcome it.
(25.08.23)

You always made your dreams seem so much smaller than everybody else's. Now, you have made one of them come true. You have seen that they are just as big as the next person's, and for yourself, bigger than you could ever imagine.
(02.09.2023)

I think I'm holding onto something I can't have.
I've noticed I do it a lot. I try to hold on to things as tightly as I can, but it's never enough. They always end up slipping from my grasp.
Why is that?
Am I so desperate for love that I will cling to the anchor sinking beneath my feet, knowing it will end in pain?
(26.01.2024)

Being angry is pretty much all I know. I've been used to feeling anger for as long as I can remember.
This? This is not something I am used to.
I miss you and I respect you and I don't blame you for anything.
I just *wish* that I could be angry at you.
These foreign feelings are overwhelming me.
Because I am used to anger. It's pretty much all I know.
(27.01.2024)

I remember when we were younger, we could never understand when the grown-ups would stay friends after they broke up.
Impossible, right?
I'd foolishly thought I'd reached that point of being a grown-up, when everything happened between us.
It felt very mature, but my childish heart couldn't understand how we could be friends but not together.
Impossible, right?
(28.01.2024)

My twenty-fifth year of life taught me a lot of things.
It taught me about toxicity, in myself and in others. It showed me what a true gentleman can look like and taught me a fair bit about my self-worth.
I fell in love with the outdoors again, and I managed to read a hundred books throughout the year.
I laughed a lot, but I cried a lot too.
All while I was surrounded by the best people, being supported to the hilt. I'm so grateful for those people who make leaving twenty-five behind so difficult, but even more grateful to those who have got me excited for twenty-six, when there was a time that I wasn't excited for my tomorrow.
(29.01.2024)

When the sun came up this morning, you took a breath.
The kind of breath that knocks on your rib cage to remind your heart that it has not stopped beating yet.
(29.01.2024)

I know you aren't dealing with this well.
We are both in the same boat and it's rocky. God, it is rocky!
But I don't want to be out at sea any more.
I want the tide to bring me in, so I can kiss the sand and say, "Thank God, I made it home."
(30.01.2024)

I feel like I'm spiralling. And I'm scared this is how it will be from now on.
(03.02.2024)

They came back.
Darker and stronger than they've ever been.
Out of nowhere when I was heading home, I cried behind the wheel, imagining driving myself into something quieter, somewhere calmer than where my mind was allowing me to be.
(04.02.2024)

No amount of quotes or manifestations can silence the voices in my head. They scream out my flaws and rip at my self-worth, leaving me in pieces.
(04.02.2024)

I always had my eyes shut the whole time, convinced that if I kept my eyes shut, it would be over faster.
That I wouldn't feel so *disgusting* afterwards.
That if I pretended I wasn't there, then I wouldn't be.
I used to think about happy films I'd seen that week or recount a memory that I was particularly fond of, just to try and block it out.
To try and block you out.
But it's impossible to hide from the devil when he is lying in the same bed as you.
(09.02.2024)

There is so much that I do that has been affected by my past without me realising.

The way I act and react in situations is a deep-rooted need to protect myself now that I have the ability to.

In arguments, I aim to hurt and shoot to kill. I need to have the last word, it makes me feel powerful and I spent way too long feeling the opposite.

The only way I know how to do that is to cut you deep; I use your lowest points to drag you down.

In that sense, I am just like him, kicking you when you are under. You do not deserve this.

I did not deserve him or the way he acted.

But I know my methods are wrong, regardless of my treatment. You deserve better.

(11.02.2024)

I have turned to medication to try and quieten my emotions, to bring them back to how they used to be.
I have acknowledged that I am no longer okay, and I have finally had the strength to ask for help.
(12.02.2024)

I am so tired.
Tired of this life.
Tired of these feelings.
But I'm scared of what would follow if I chose to avoid my problems and give in to the slumber.
(02.03.2024)

I've started therapy. I had to.
I can't go on with this noise inside my head.
I can't go on feeling like any day could be my last.
(07.03.2024)

When I was fourteen, you had the audacity to tell me over the family dinner table that I was a slag.

You said to me that because I smiled at boys – I was going to end up pregnant, with no job at sixteen. A failure.

Look at me now. I am twenty-six years old, and thanks to you, I find it so difficult to love myself.

How can I expect anybody else to?

(20.04.2024)

I was eleven.

I was eleven and you took advantage of my innocence and my trust. You were sixty-two.

You were sixty-two and someone I was taught to rely on. How was I ever meant to survive against those odds?

You were old enough to know better, to know that you were ruining me.

I was too young to understand what cum was. I didn't know what it was and why it was in my mouth after you made me do that thing that I didn't like doing.

That thing that I didn't like doing when you got me alone in the dark loft, away from everyone downstairs.

Alone in the dark loft, away from everyone downstairs, I couldn't understand why you always got me on my own. Why did you prefer it when it was just you and I?

I was eleven, and you took away my innocence and my trust. You were sixty-two.

(23.04.2024)

How are we so similar? How can I look at you and, without speaking any words, you know what I'm thinking? You are making quite a dark time that little bit easier and I can't think of a way to show you how thankful I am for shining a light.
(24.04.2024)

I sometimes wonder why you chose me. I'm curious to know if it was age, appearance or access to me that swayed you to make the choices you made.
It's something I'll never understand, which I guess gives me another thing to hate you for.
(25.04.2024)

There was so much anger in everything I had written up until this point. There will continue to be anger, but now I have an idea of why it's there.
You.
You took so much from me. You made me grow up way before my time, and then you died. Leaving me to try and fix a mess that never, ever should have been made.
You have made me into a monster, and you don't even get to see the person you created.
(26.04.2024)

You must have had some balls to know that you didn't even have to tell me to keep it a secret.
Did you already know the shame would shut me up and eat me alive for fourteen years after that?
(28.04.2024)

I'm scared it's too good to be true. I'm scared you will soon see sense and leave, like everybody else has.
I'm scared you deserve more than the broken pieces I can offer you.
(29.04.2024)

Something came up in my photos on my phone today, as a 'memory'.
It was the little black book you kept, where you wrote down every 'bad' thing we did as children.
Out of a list of twenty-one, my name is on there *sixteen* times. I was five.
It makes me wonder, how long were you keeping an eye on me before you chose to destroy my childhood?
(30.04.2024)

It was *not* okay back then.
It should *not* have been the norm. Boys will *not* be boys.
Get these notions out of your head.
If it was normal, why do they get you on your own and isolate you from the ones who care about you?
They know they've done wrong; they just don't care. It was not okay, and it *never* will be.
(01.05.24)

How many people must be suffering in silence, afraid that the truth will alienate them from the lives they have come to know? All because their monsters couldn't stay concealed under their beds or in their closets. They climbed out of their hiding places, slid under our sheets and surrounded us.
Scaring us into silence for years.
(02.05.24)

I am so sick of hearing that boys will be boys, that it's 'just what happened' in those days and that they were desensitised after it happened for so long.
People should be shouting until their lungs are empty and their throats are raw that 'no' means 'no'.
(04.05.2024)

How lucky I am to have people who will guide me when I am lost. Bringing me out of this darkness and into their light. (04.05.2024)

Why do you keep trying to force away the one thing you want to hold close? Soon he will realise.
He will see you as the broken and cruel girl you were made to be.
He will see goodness in others that you cannot even comprehend, and then, he will leave.
(05.05.2024)

The sun pushed the clouds out of the way for long enough today that the flowers reached up to touch the sky, reminding us all that there is beauty.
(07.05.2024)

And when that panic sets in.
When the darkness gets to be far more than you think you can survive. Remember, that no matter how strongly you feel it, you are not alone.
(09.05.2024)

You had so much confidence in what you were doing.
You were so sure I would never scream, that you lay in the bottom bunk of our bed with my sister above us while you put your head between my tiny thighs.
I hated it.
I hated you.
I hated myself.
I remember thinking, 'slug'. I distinctly recall comparing the horror of what you were subjecting me to, to what a slug felt like.
But how was I to stop you when I couldn't say what it was you were doing to me right beneath her?
I didn't understand it, but I knew enough to know it was wrong.
I was scared and uneasy, so I laughed.
You pinched my legs hard to try and keep me silent, but the spell was broken. She asked, "What are you doing down there?"
I said, "He's tickling me."
Only these tickles, were like razor-sharp claws gouging out parts of myself I hadn't even realised I could lose yet.
(10.05.2024)

We are more than a statistic. We are women, men and children trying to stumble our way through this thing they call healing. *They* are more than a statistic. They are guardians, family, friends and strangers, who are breaking us into the pieces that we are now so desperately trying to hold together.
(12.05.2024)

I remember how uncomfortable you made me when you used to lie with me before bed. Your hands always landed in places I didn't want them to go.
They crawled under my nightie, slipped past my underwear – they had the days of the week on them – and ripped away any sense of safety I may have felt before.
That night was a Tuesday.
(13.05.2024)

Talking has helped. Talking has ignited something in me that I might have feared before. It has lit a match for *hope*.
For myself and for others like me.
I want to be there, for all those who aren't sure how to survive the darkness. I want to be there for them holding the flame.
(15.05.2024)

You used to put it on the telly.
The first time you acted shocked when you said, "Don't tell me you haven't learnt about this yet."
I wonder, how *exactly* did you expect that to go?
Was it your intention to frighten me so much that I tried to hide in the toilet until Mum came home? Only for you to stand on the other side ordering me to come out.
I was too scared to move so I stayed put, but the lock was easily bypassed with a coin. When you opened the door, you made it sound like you were sorry,
But you made me carry on watching anyway.
(16.05.2024)

Admitting it to yourself, in my opinion, is by far the hardest part of healing. You may have built walls so high that you can't see the top of them any more.
But slowly, you can break them down, brick by brick, and we, the others, will be on the other side waiting for you.
(17.05.2024)

I realised today, whilst looking through photos that when I was eleven – the age that you so easily crushed my innocence – I was a bridesmaid at your wedding.
I walked down the aisle behind you both and stood by your side in pictures. It was so long ago that I can't remember if it was before or after the abuse.
I am worried now that how I remembered it, isn't how it happened.
Surely, I've got it wrong, because if I *was* eleven, then you actively chose to shatter the magic that *should* have surrounded that day. Tainting *my* memories of people who had no idea of what depravities you were hiding.
(18.05.2024)

I couldn't have a man's dick in my mouth for the longest time.
Anytime, I would go near one I would freeze.
I didn't realise at the time that it was PTSD.
The memory of your rough hands holding my head down until I couldn't breathe any more was plaguing my thoughts.
It took years for me not to think twice about it.
Yet, I still freak out when someone puts their hands in my hair.
(19.05.2024)

I hope that when I have children the world is kinder.
I hope they will never know the blinding fear of not being heard when they say no. I don't want them to experience their bed sinking from the weight of the unwanted.
I long for them to love openly, without fear, and for the feelings to be reciprocated in healthy ways.
I wish for them to have the childhood that I didn't get.
(21.05.2024)

You are so strong. You survived the attack against your innocence. I promise you, you can survive taking control of your life again.
(24.05.2024)

The best way to describe the coping mechanism that I, and many others have used is that there is a river flowing downstream.
It holds all of your emotions and memories, good and bad.
We – as children – to try and survive, built a wall across the banks. A huge wall to shield us from painful thoughts and feelings – to protect us from the things we did not understand. But the river didn't know that it was supposed to stop flowing, and without the ability to stop, it carried on.
What we have done – by opening up this many years later – is break down that dam that we so bravely built in our youth.
And in its place, years and years of unpleasantness are surging through, overflowing and flooding the riverbanks, coming out in angry bursts.
Soon, I can't say exactly when, but the river will return to its usual height. It will flow gently through you instead of feeling like it's dragging you under and drowning you.
(25.05.2024)

I understand that you are scared, but is the darkness suffocating you not far scarier than the idea of being pulled into the light? Can it possibly get any worse than how you are feeling right now?
(26.05.2024)

It took me a long time to realise that the truth I shared didn't just affect me. It took me months of naivety to think I was the only one hurting.
I shook the very foundation we built our family lives on.
I selfishly believed that they had no right to their anger or sadness because it happened to me and not to them.
I didn't think about the fact that they had to grieve the past and the man they believed to have known.
To grieve the innocence that was taken from me and the pain I had to live through.
(27.05.2024)

They took so much from us when we were too young to understand.
Do not let them continue to take all of the good things from us now that they are gone.
(31.05.2024)

I wish I could explain the void I am feeling. Empty without being empty,
Silent, but it feels busy inside my head. Unhappy, happy, numb.
I can't figure it out, so how is anyone else meant to?
(01.06.2024)

I can't see myself moving forward.
I am comparing myself to others and their achievements while I sit motionless.
Waiting for better days.
I cannot see a future in myself and it scares me.
(02.06.2024)

I remember being frozen, with shame and fear.
Always in a fight with myself about whether to say something or to keep quiet. I never did have the courage to stand up to you.
(03.06.2024)

Do not take my medication for weakness.
I have a strength in me that keeps me grounded.
I am working through things that you could not even imagine.
(10.06.2024)

I think I am many things; I call myself many things.
Most of them are from my personal arsenal made on the days I dislike myself. However, I have recently come to realise that I am strong, I am resilient and I am determined to get through everything that has been thrown at me. Regardless of all the traumas that I have lived through, I am *still* here. I am *still* smiling.
(12.06.2024)

The sun is always in the sky, even when you can't see it through the clouds. It will always be there, we just have to be patient and remember: *'That it cannot always be cloudy'*.
(14.06.2024)

I am so proud of you.
You thank me for helping you, but I have merely reminded you of the things that have been so easily forgotten.
You are strong.
You are safe.
And he cannot hurt you any more.
I am proud of the way you have handled the abundance of emotions that have hit you recently, I know it hasn't been easy. But I will be here, holding your hand the entire way.
(15.06.24)

For all of those who had fathers that took their title for granted. For those whose fathers took their power and tried to destroy the goodness so obviously in our young souls.
Today could be a painful day for you, for us, but know that I am here, and I will hold your hands through every post and every card, professing the greatness of fathers we did not get to experience.
Father's Day (16.06.2024)

Today, I am grateful that I no longer have to pretend my father was a great man. Telling people my truth has made today easier. He was not a great man.
I don't even think he was a good man.
But me? I am fantastic, no thanks to him and *all* thanks to me.
(17.06.2024)

You make me feel safe.
(18.06.2024)

An arrow can only be shot by pulling it backwards.
When life is dragging you down, it just means that it's going to launch you into something great.
The weight you feel on your shoulders is just your body subconsciously getting ready to jump into action.
The heaviness of your heart only makes your mind strive for the love it deserves. And you deserve it all.
(21.06.2024)

You see no issues in the way you have handled this situation.
With spite and unkindness pouring out of you.
I ask, if your daughter was dragged into a situation the mirror image of this, would you be pleased with how she was treated?
Rather, would you stand by the childish notion that they were right to ambush and attack '*her*' out of the blue?
If you would, you are more far gone than I had realised and glad that I have removed you from my life.
(11.07.2024)

No longer can I justify your behaviour with 'oh but that's just what he's like'.
It would be unfair to myself and to others, to continue ignoring the actions that you take. You need to be held accountable for the choices you make and the people you hurt.
(03.08.2024)

Allegedly, you only intervened as you were worried for me, concerned that I would be hurt by the fallout.
Little did we know, *you were* the fallout. You were hurting me with the choices you were making.
(04.08.2024)

Again, the darkness slips into my mind like a past lover, crawling under the sheets. Whispering the lies of my worst hours, in an attempt to break me down.
And I am so scared that it might be working.
(07.08.2024)

The pride that fills me when I see how far you have come almost overwhelms me.
You have not let him control your life, instead you have found a man who loves you for you and plans to do so forever.
Cherish that, and cherish yourself for the progress you have made.
(10.08.2024)

Of course, my answer would be 'yes'.
You have stood by me through some of my darkest days and it would be my absolute pleasure to stand by you on the lightest of yours.
An honour, some would say.
(11.08.2024)

Loss, regardless of how small, can hurt more than you might expect, but it is something you are capable of weathering. You have done it before; you can surely do it again. (13.08.2024)

I don't think I can keep pretending like everything is okay.
I cannot shake the sadness that seems to surround me from the
moment I wake up until the moment I fall asleep.
(15.08.2024)

Everything is so dark.
There isn't the usual chaos in my mind at the moment, it is silent. And the silence scares me.
I am used to navigating the shouts and screams in my head, barely able to hear myself think. If they aren't there, is there anything left to try and fight for?
(19.08.2024)

I think I'm scaring the ones who care about me.
They keep gently pushing me to shake myself off and get up like I have in the past. But I can't bring myself to my knees, let alone stand.
I can't fight the silence and darkness that is suffocating me.
I am scaring myself, and I don't know how to protect the ones who love me from the consequences.
(20.08.2024)

If you're driving one hundred and twenty miles an hour down the motorway, it's quite likely that you're going to crash. People will try and warn you; they'll flash their lights and beep their horns, desperate to tell you that the road is not as long as you had first thought.
When you inevitably crash, all that's left, after the rubble, the smoke and the hurt, is nothing.
That's the best way I can describe the breakdown I've recently had. I was moving so fast that I didn't even realise my road was running out. I didn't realise that I had people trying to warn me to slow down, and once I crashed, there was nothing. After being accustomed to moving so fast for so long, I felt numb when I crashed and was met with absolutely nothing.
Just a darkness that enveloped me, sealing me off from the outside world with a gentle kiss. Teasing me into a pit, promising secrets too dark to admit.
(21.09.2024)

I am proud of myself for the progress I have made this year. Admittedly, I've had two mental health breakdowns, but the difference between the two has been striking.
I have grown. I continue to grow. I am becoming the person he was always scared I would be.
(26.09.2024)

This life is a little like stumbling around in the dark. Not knowing which way to turn and what might be waiting for you around the corner.

We find people along the way, and they gain our trust, as we do theirs. These people have light in their souls to help guide us along the unknown paths. Some of them may lose their way, their lights may dim or they may just decide that the way you're going isn't where they want to follow.

As survivors, the dark is a scary place to be. That's where the secrets are hidden. That's where the elongated fingers of our past emerge from the shadows, rip at our ankles and try to drag us back to where they think we belong. Where they have put us. But we won't let them. We *can't* let them.

It's scary. I don't think it will ever not be scary, trying to figure out how to navigate the right way in the dark. But we are here, we have survived and we can stand as one.

Uniting each of our lights to banish the darkness, even if it is just for a moment.

(29.09.2024)

Some days are good and some days are bad.
Unfortunately, we can't know for sure which it will be until we have woken up from the night.
And that right there is reason enough to ensure you keep waking up, to keep on keeping on.
The start of a good day could be just what you needed to pull through.
(30.09.2024)

Healing and coping. They aren't so different, are they?
I thought I was fine—healed—for the longest time until I admitted to myself that I was barely coping.
I was using alcohol and a toxic relationship as a crutch. Now, I am healing.
I am putting myself first and listening to my body.
I haven't turned to drugs or anything darker or more dangerous, despite the ease in which I could have.
There is no judgement.
It's so hard trying to be strong all the time. Sometimes we need something to soften the blows.
(02.10.2024)

They all said we were in the honeymoon phase at the start. Said it wouldn't last.
So I pinned my happiness down to us being new to each other; learning what the other liked, disliked, feared and believed.
We've managed six months and we are *still* learning.
I am still learning.
But one thing I do know is that we are good together, regardless of any phases.
(05.10.2024)

She was just a girl.
A girl that grew up with the toxic attention and intentions from others.
A girl that has experienced incredibly tumultuous events in her twenty-six years.
A girl that has struggled to regulate her emotions and differentiate the big feelings that drown her.
I am just a girl, who, along with around *one* in *six* other children were sexually abused by someone they were taught to trust.
(09.10.24)

Every time I feel like I've got my life together, something comes along and knocks me off balance. Kind of like walking into a low-hanging branch when you are looking at the floor. It smacks you in the face and leaves you confused, swinging your head around to see where the assault came from.
When I was knocked off balance, I wish someone was there to tell me what I'm about to tell you:
Man, fuck that branch!
It's left you disorientated, it's disrupted your flow and you are absolutely allowed to be mad about it.
Feel your feelings, no matter how big. Don't try to ignore them, because as much as it seems like it'll help in the moment, it won't. You have people who support you. Feeling the feelings is a scary thing, but it will help in the long run. I promise.
Don't push yourself before you are ready, you will only exhaust yourself with the pressure, mentally and physically.
Contrary to belief, when you feel sad and you want to wallow, you don't need to 'get up, get out of bed and get outside'. You don't need to 'move your body and go and see friends'. It doesn't always help, and it's okay to admit that.
Feel those feelings. When you have a small positive, any slight improvement; ease up on yourself, make a coffee, sit by the window to feel the sun on your face.
There is no shame in needing to take time to heal.
Feel the feelings. The bad ones are intense, but the good ones are sure to follow. I promise.
(10.10.2024)